The Little Prince

This book belongs to :

Manufactured by Amazon.ca
Bolton, ON

15820707R00068